Exploring the Intricacies of Data Analytics

Nishant Baxi

pencil

ISBN 978-93-5883-111-5
© Nishant Baxi 2023

Published in India 2023 by Pencil

A brand of
One Point Six Technologies Pvt. Ltd.
Unit no. 26, Ground Floor, Building A1,
Wadala Truck Terminal Road,
Near Post Office, Antop Hill, Mumbai - 400037
E connect@thepencilapp.com
W www.thepencilapp.com

DISCLAIMER: *The opinions expressed in this book are those of the authors and do not purport to reflect the views of the Publisher.*

Author biography

I am an experienced content creator and digital/social media marketing professional with a demonstrated history of working in the publishing industry. I am skilled in E-Learning, Market Research, Online Advertising, Management, and Business Development, Content Development.

CONTENTS

Preface

Throughout this ebook, any complicated terms or jargon will be explained in layman's terms to ensure the material remains accessible and comprehensible. The goal is to provide a comprehensive overview of Data Analytics that serves as a useful introduction for those new to the field, as well as a handy reference for more experienced analysts.

Introduction

Definition of Data Analytics

Data analytics is a broad term used to refer to the process of examining, cleansing, transforming, and modeling data sets to discover useful information and support decision-making. This complex discipline encompasses a variety of techniques and theories drawn from many fields within the broad context of mathematics, statistics, computer science, and information science (Suthaharan, 2016).

Data analytics techniques are generally divided into four types: descriptive analytics, diagnostic analytics, predictive analytics, and prescriptive analytics. Descriptive analytics involves analyzing historical data to identify patterns and trends; this is often used in business intelligence. Diagnostic analytics seeks to identify the causes of a particular outcome. Predictive analytics uses statistical models and algorithms to predict future outcomes based on historical data, while prescriptive analytics employs optimization and simulation techniques to advise on the possible outcomes (Sharda, Delen & Turban, 2017).

The goal of data analytics is to generate insights that can be used to improve the performance of an organization or system. This is done by identifying patterns, relationships, and trends in the data, and using this information to make informed decisions. This process can be used in many industries, such as healthcare, retail, finance, among others.

The process of data analytics often begins with data gathering from various sources. This may include structured data, such as databases, and unstructured data, such as text files or social media posts. Data cleansing is then performed to remove errors, inconsistencies, and inaccuracies. The cleansed data is then analyzed using statistical and data mining techniques. Finally, the results are interpreted and communicated through data visualization tools, reports, or dashboards (Fayyad, Piatetsky-Shapiro & Smyth, 1996).

The ever-increasing power of computing and the proliferation of digital technologies have made data analytics a central feature of modern organizations. With the capacity to analyze large volumes of complex data, organizations can gain a competitive edge, identify new opportunities, enhance productivity, and make data-driven decisions.

Notwithstanding, there are also challenges inherent in the field of data analytics. Security, privacy, and ethical concerns are among the significant issues that need to be addressed. Moreover, the complexities of data analytics require skilled professionals who can understand and apply the appropriate techniques and tools.

In conclusion, data analytics is a powerful tool for extracting value from data. It involves collecting, cleaning, analyzing, and interpreting data to understand past performance, guide current actions, and predict future outcomes.

Importance and relevance of Data Analytics in today's big data environment

The modern age is characterized by an unprecedented surge in digital information known as big data, which is straining the traditional ways of managing, processing, and making sense of this information (Manyika et al., 2011). The significance of data analytics in understanding big data becomes evident when considering the immense amounts of data generated every day, which necessitates organization, interpretation, and application for driving insightful decision-making.

Data analytics is the discipline that encompasses the quantitative and qualitative techniques employed to enhance productivity and business gain. As defined, data is unprocessed information that becomes valuable only when analyzed (Davenport, 2013). Therefore, this article underscores the importance and relevance of data analytics in the big data environment.

The first value of data analytics lies in its capability to provide useful insights from big data. Increasingly, organizations are leveraging data analytics to understand their operations, customer feedback, and market trends, and to identify business opportunities and threats. This pivotal role of data analytics ushers in strategic knowledge that may not be readily visible in the raw data (LaValle et al., 2011).

Secondly, data analytics enables productivity and efficiency improvements. By analyzing operational data, businesses can identify inefficiencies and bottlenecks in their workflow. For instance, data analytics assists companies in identifying performance gaps, staff productivity, and resource allocation (Chen, Chiang & Storey, 2012). This key feature assists in decision-making processes related to business growth and streamlining operations for maximum efficiencies.

Thirdly, data analytics plays a crucial role in risk management. Organizations can use predictive analysis to foresee potential threats and mitigate them in a timely fashion, reducing their risks and vulnerabilities. Thus, data analytics grants them the ability to devise effective contingency plans (Davenport, 2013).

Lastly, data analytics is at the heart of innovation and competitiveness in the modern business landscape. Through the analysis of consumer trends, business analytics fosters the development of new products and services tailored to customer needs, thereby enhancing competitiveness (LaValle et al., 2011).

In conclusion, data analytics is not a mere option but an imperative in today's big data environment. Its ability to extract practical insights, improve productivity, mitigate risks, and foster innovation reaffirms its relevance and importance in various sectors. As the big data trend continues to gain momentum, businesses investing in data analytics will most likely emerge victorious in the competitive market.

Objective and scope of the ebook

The field of data analytics is an evolving landscape, with intricacies that demand a well-defined understanding for effective operationalization in today's digitized businesses. Data analytics refers to the process of examining, cleansing, transforming, and modeling data to uncover meaningful information, draw conclusions, support decision-making, and provide valuable insight into business operations.

Data analytics is an integral part of modern businesses, driving strategic planning, execution, and performance evaluation. It operates across a broad spectrum, from describing what has happened, diagnosing why it happened, and predicting what might happen in the future, to prescriptively outlining the best course of action using elaborate algorithms and machine learning techniques.

One of the key intricacies is identifying the appropriate types of data analytics to apply. The four main types are descriptive, diagnostic, predictive, and prescriptive analytics. Each type serves a different purpose and provides different insights, illustrating the complexity and multifaceted nature of data analytics.

Another critical aspect involves data quality, which is fundamental to successful data analytics. Diverse sources of data can have varying levels of quality, demanding rigorous data cleaning and validation methods. This often involves complex data transformation processes and normalization techniques, further elevating the intricacies involved.

Data analysts also face challenges related to data security and privacy regulations, like the General Data Protection Regulation (GDPR) and California Consumer Privacy Act (CCPA). Thus, understanding the legal environment surrounding data usage, applying appropriate security measures, and achieving regulatory compliance are intricate elements of practicing data analytics.

Algorithm development represents another compelling facet of data analytics. With the rapid advancements in machine learning and artificial intelligence, creating accurate and efficient algorithms is pivotal. This demands a deep understanding of various programming languages, machine learning models, and artificial intelligence concepts, demonstrating the technical complexities involved.

Lastly, dealing with Big Data—vast volumes of structured and unstructured data that inundate businesses daily—adds a level of complexity. It involves issues of storage, analysis, manipulation, and visualization that require specific tools and techniques to manage effectively.

In conclusion, exploring the intricacies of data analytics unveils a complex yet rewarding field. It demands a multifaceted skill set, ranging from technical prowess in programming and machine learning to an intuitive understanding of business operations, sophisticated analytical competency, and a firm grasp of the legal landscape surrounding data use.

In an increasingly data-driven world, possessing a solid understanding of these intricacies can unlock significant potential for businesses, helping them make informed decisions, enhance operational efficiency, drive profitability, and gain a competitive edge.

Chapter 1 Understanding Data Analytics

The Evolution of Data Analytics

Data Analytics refers to the process of inspecting, cleaning, transforming, and modeling data to discover useful information, suggest conclusions, and support decision-making. The evolution of data analytics can be traced back to the 1960s when a statistician would use mathematical models to predict future outcomes or behaviors with a scientific approach (Sanders & Courtney, 1985). In this era, the methodologies were unsophisticated and depended on procedures that were generally executed by hand.

The 1980s marked a new era in data analytics with the introduction of personal computers enhancing the ability to gather, analyze, and disseminate enormous amounts of information manually (Kobsa, 2001). This revolution improved data analysis methods and brought a degree of speed that was not previously realized, enabling analysts to arrive at conclusions more effectively and efficiently.

The start of the 21st century brought about a digital revolution causing the amount of data generated to grow exponentially. The explosion of data made possible by the proliferation of internet connectivity, the advancement of digital technologies, and the birth of social media platforms led to the concept of 'Big Data' (Manyika et al., 2011). The growth of big data led to the emergence of advanced analytic techniques like data mining, machine learning, and predictive analytics.

With the advancement of technology, data analytics has evolved into more specific fields including business intelligence, predictive analytics, and machine learning, just to name a few (Davenport & Harris, 2007). Today, data analytics platforms harness algorithms to analyze structured and unstructured data to drive a wide range of applications ranging from business intelligence to healthcare diagnostics, security intelligence, and marketing (Waller & Fawcett, 2013).

In conclusion, the evolution of data analytics has revolutionized how businesses, government institutions, and individuals make decisions. With the world becoming increasingly digital and interconnected, the future of data analytics promises even more sophisticated capabilities, driven by advancements in artificial intelligence and machine learning technologies.

An overview of the Data Analytics process

To embrace the digital revolution, organizations are increasingly turning to data analytics as a means to extract valuable insights from an abundance of structured and unstructured data. Effective management, interpretation, and application of data are imperative in today's data-driven business world. This article provides an overview of the data analytics process, integral to unlocking the potential offered by vast quantities of data.

Data analytics refers to the science of examining raw data to draw insights about that information (Davenport & Harris, 2007). The process of data analytics is multifaceted, involving various techniques and theories drawn from mathematics, statistics, computer programming, and business management, among others.

The data analytics process can generally be divided into five main stages.

1. Data Collection: The initial step involves acquiring data from various sources, including databases, social media, IoT devices, and other data-generating platforms (Kelleher & Tierney, 2018).

2. Data Processing: Once collected, the raw data is then processed and organized for analysis. This often entails data cleansing, integration, and transformation to ensure that the data is accurate, uniform, and readily analyzable.

3. Data Analysis: The third step involves the application of statistical and mathematical models to the processed data. This enables analysts to identify trends, patterns, and relationships within the data, contributing to sound decision-making.

4. Data Visualization: In the fourth stage, findings from the data analysis are presented in an understandable and visually appealing format, via reports, dashboards, graphs, or charts. This aids in the communication of complex data insights (Few, 2009).

5. Data Interpretation: Finally, the conclusions drawn from the analysis need to be interpreted and made actionable. Data interpretation involves deciphering the complex meanings of the statistical outcomes, deriving insights, and using these findings to shape tactical and strategic business decisions (Provost & Fawcett, 2013).

Undoubtedly, data analytics has become a critical component in driving business strategy and operational efficiency. As businesses continue to navigate today's data-rich environment, the role and importance of the data analytics process will only grow.

In conclusion, the data analytics process provides a structured approach for managing and interpreting vast amounts of data. Whether in business operations, customer behavior analysis, or strategic decision-making, this process equips organizations with the much-needed skills and tools to thrive in an increasingly data-driven world.

Various types of Data Analytics: Descriptive, Diagnostic, Predictive, and Prescriptive

In the data-driven world of today, deep and meaningful insights are derived from raw data through a process called data analytics. Data analytics can be categorized into four main types: Descriptive, Diagnostic, Predictive, and Prescriptive (LaValle et al., 2011).

Descriptive Analytics, as the name suggests, helps in understanding and describing historical trends and patterns. It performs a historical data analysis to provide answers to questions like what happened, or how frequently it occurred. It utilizes data aggregation and data mining techniques to provide insights into the past and is a very common type of business analytics used by organizations (Davenport, 2013).

Diagnostic Analytics goes a step further than the Descriptive Analytics and attempts to understand why something happened. It looks at patterns and trends to identify the root causes of an event. Diagnostic Analytics is accomplished using techniques including drill-down, data discovery, data mining, and correlations.

Predictive Analytics, on the other hand, uses statistical models and forecasting techniques to discern and interpret what could happen in the future. It is characterized by using historical data to predict future outcomes. Predictive analytics can help organizations anticipate future trends, behavior, and events (Munroe et al., 2017).

The highest order of data analytics is the Prescriptive Analytics. As the name implies, it prescribes what actions need to be taken to maximize or achieve a specific goal. It uses optimization and simulation algorithms alongside business rules to provide advice on decision-making. It is particularly important as it moves beyond just reporting data to suggest actions that can shape future outcomes (Davenport & Harris, 2007).

In conclusion, these four types of data analytics each have a different purpose: Descriptive Analytics helps companies understand what has happened in the past, Diagnostic Analytics explains why it happened, Predictive Analytics forecasts what might happen in the future, and Prescriptive Analytics advises on achieving the best possible outcomes. Hence, to harness the full potential of data, organizations need to apply these different types of data analytics judiciously.

Chapter 2 The Tools and Techniques of Data Analytics

Introduction to common tools in Data Analytics – Excel, SQL, R, Python, SAS

The field of data analytics is littered with a plethora of tools that offer specific functionalities to address diverse analytical tasks. The choice of these tools depends on the needs and the level of complexity involved in the task. Among these, the most popular ones remain Excel, SQL, R, Python, and SAS.

Microsoft Excel, though a basic tool, is powerful for several reasons. Excel allows users to organize data in tabular formats, provides simple and straightforward functions for basic statistical analysis, supports visual data analysis such as charts and graphs, and comes in handy for conducting quick data sweeps and preliminary analysis (Microsoft, 2021).

Structured Query Language (SQL), on the other hand, is the go-to tool for handling and manipulating structured data stored in databases. It provides the ability to extract and present data in the desired format. SQL is essential for tasks that involve complex querying, data manipulation, data aggregation and joins from multiple tables (IBM, 2021).

R, a language and environment for statistical computing and graphics, is free software that provides a wide variety of statistical techniques. Its benefits include data handling and storage, calculations on arrays, tools for data analysis, and graphical facilities for data visualization (R Project, 2021).

Python, an interpreted, object-oriented, and high-level programming language, is also a popular tool in data analytics. Its design philosophy emphasizes code readability, and its syntax allows programmers to express concepts in fewer lines of code than might be possible in languages such as C++ or Java (Python Software Foundation, 2021). Python is hailed for its comprehensive data analysis libraries like NumPy, pandas, and SciPy.

Lastly, Statistical Analysis System (SAS) is another important tool used in large-scale data analytics. SAS is an integrated system of software products, primarily used for data management and advanced analytics. Its primary features include data mining, report writing, statistical analysis, business planning, and predictive analytics (SAS Institute Inc., 2021).

While there are numerous tools available for data analytics, these five remain among the most common and popular choices. Each tool has its strengths, and the best tool often depends on the requirements, complexity of data, and the specific task at hand.

Description and comparison of different Data Analytics techniques – Data mining, Machine Learning, Neural

Data analytics has revolutionized the way companies and organizations analyze information, influence rational decisions, and predict accurate outcomes. The sphere of data analytics employs a variety of methods and techniques, but this article will primarily focus on data mining, machine learning, and neural networks.

Data Mining refers to the computational process of discovering patterns in large data sets. The primary goal of data mining is to extract valuable information from these complex data sets, and then convert it into an understandable and usable structure. Data mining has a broad application spectrum including financial services, marketing, retail, telecom, and healthcare, among others [1].

Machine Learning, a subset of artificial intelligence (AI), enables systems to automatically learn from previous experiences and improve performance without explicitly being programmed. This learning is based on the recognition of complex patterns in millions of data. Machine learning is vital in areas such as product recommendation, image recognition, and predictive maintenance.

On the other hand, Neural Networks are algorithms mimicking the human brain, designed to recognize patterns. They interpret data through the lens of machine perception, clustering raw input, and recognizing patterns therein. Neural networks are extensively used in applications like speech recognition, image recognition, and natural language processing [2].

In comparing these techniques, they all offer the benefits of improved accuracy and decision-making capabilities in their specific application domains. However, their operations differ significantly.

Data mining primarily focuses on the discovery of previously unknown relationships among the data. The process involves pre-processing, data cleaning, data transformation, model evaluation, and knowledge representation. It requires human intervention and prior knowledge of the domain to form the hypnosis.

Contrastingly, machine learning emphasizes learning from the data and making predictions. It operates by training an algorithm using labeled data (supervised learning), or discovering hidden patterns from unlabeled data (unsupervised learning) [3]. Unlike data mining, machine learning can learn and evolve with experience over time.

Neural Networks, meanwhile, are designed to biologically simulate the workings of the human brain, aiming to replicate its ability to learn. Neural networks analyze multiple inputs and assign respective weights, which are then fine-tuned over numerous iterations.

In essence, while there is a connection and interplay between these data analytics techniques, they operate differently and offer distinct advantages depending upon their application.

Understanding these differences is fundamental for businesses and data scientists to ensure they choose the optimal technique that best aligns with their specific strategic goals and data characteristics. This is further augmented by the rapid technological advancements and vast amounts of data generated daily, necessitating the use of data analytics techniques more reliably.

Chapter 3 Data Analytics and Database Management

Understanding the relationship between Data Analytics and Database Management

In the rapidly evolving world of technology, two concepts that have gained tremendous importance in the business sphere are data analytics and database management. They are distinctly different concepts, but they possess a profound intertwining relationship that aids in the advancement of data-based decision-making.

Database management is a comprehensive system that facilitates the creation, management, and administration of databases. It allows organizations to systematically store, organize, protect, and retrieve their valuable data. The adoption of a reliable database management system (DBMS) eliminates the complexities associated with data handling, ensuring data integrity and security. It also considerably enhances the operational efficiency of businesses (Rahman, 2015).

On the other hand, data analytics involves the examination of raw data to derive meaningful insights. This complex process utilizes specialized systems and software to convert unintelligible data into understandable information that can guide strategic business decisions. Consequently, it aids in identifying patterns, predicting future trends, and informing strategic planning.

Understanding the relationship between these two concepts involves acknowledging how database management serves as the backbone for successful data analytics. The DBMS provides the structured data necessary for data analytics. It houses the data that are subjected to rigorous analysis, and as such, the efficiency and reliability of a DBMS directly reflect on the quality of insights derived from data analysis. The importance of this relationship is ever more apparent in the age of Big Data, where organizations continuously handle copious amounts of data that must be efficiently managed and analyzed for strategic advantages (Kumar & Khilari, 2016).

Moreover, the harmonious integration of database management and data analytics has given rise to innovative technological solutions. One remarkable example is the advent of real-time analytics. As the data stored in databases become immediately available for analysis, organizations can promptly react to changes, significantly improving their business responsiveness.

Ultimately, the symbiotic relationship between data analytics and database management maximizes data utilization, enhancing the decision-making process. In the face of a digital future, understanding this relationship is crucial for businesses looking to leverage data as a strategic asset.

Importance of proper Data Management in Data Analytics

Data analytics has become a pivotal aspect of running a successful business in recent times. It involves perusing and examining large datasets to extract actionable insights, facilitating well-informed decision-making. However, the efficacy of data analytics heavily relies on one fundamental aspect: proper data management (Katal, Wazid & Goudar, 2013). Without efficient data management practices, an organization's data may remain chaotic, leading to inaccuracies and inefficiencies in data analytics processes.

Effective data management begins with implementing procedures and policies that govern data collection. Since data quality is crucial for accurate analytics, collected data should be clean, detailed, and suitably formatted (Wixom, et al., 2014). This necessitates data validation and removal of duplicates, ensuring that erroneous or misleading data doesn't compromise the data analytics process. Furthermore, robust data management entails maintaining a catalog of collected data, classified appropriately for easy retrieval.

Consistent data management reduces redundancy. It eliminates multiple versions of datasets, enhancing data integrity and efficiency. Through centralized data management, businesses can ensure consistent data usage across the organization, maintaining unity in reporting and decision-making processes. Standardized data promotes the production of precise, consistent reports and analyses from the collected data (Wixom, et al., 2014).

Proper data management also paves the way for data security, a paramount concern in the digital age where data breaches are a persisting threat. Organizations can deploy data encryption, control access, and conduct regular audits to ensure data safety. Without such measures, sensitive data may fall into the wrong hands, leading to repercussions ranging from financial losses to reputational damage (Jayakody & Raman, 2018).

Finally, proper data management supports regulatory compliance. With regulatory bodies enforcing stringent data handling and privacy regulations, businesses must ensure that data is properly managed, safeguarded, and used ethically (Jayakody & Raman, 2018). Appropriate data management practices demonstrate compliance with these norms, bypassing hefty penalties and preserving consumer trust.

In conclusion, the importance of proper data management within data analytics cannot be understated. It establishes the foundation for successful data analytics, ensures data reliability, streamlines processes, preserves data security, and underlines regulatory compliance. Therefore, organizations aspiring to derive meaningful insights from their data should prioritize robust data management mechanisms.

Exploration of Database Management Systems (DBMS) used in Data Analytics

Data Analytics utilizes various Database Management Systems (DBMS) to turn unstructured data into comprehensive information. DBMS's fundamental function in Data Analytics is to enable secure data management and create a systematic environment for easy data retrieval (Zhao, 2019).

One of the widely used DBMS in Data Analytics is Oracle Database. Oracle remains a dominant player in the DBMS market with features like Real Application Testing, Total Recall, and Automatic Memory Management, which aid in comprehensive data analytics. Also, Oracle provides scalability and ensures the efficient handling of voluminous data in real-time analysis (Oracle, 2021).

Another prominent DBMS used in Data Analytics is Microsoft SQL Server. It provides comprehensive security features, robust data compression, and efficient scalability, making it suitable for analytics. The SQL Server Analysis Services (SSAS) is an essential MS SQL tool crucial in the analysis and visualization of data in business analytics (Microsoft, 2021).

Despite several of these proprietary systems in place, open-source platforms like MySQL also display considerable strength in data analytics. MySQL supports substantial concurrent connections, utilizes memory efficiently, and supports multithreading. Its compatibility with various platforms and support for major programming languages makes MySQL a practical choice for analytics-heavy applications (MySQL, 2021).

Notably, PostgreSQL has also gained popularity in data analytics. It supports both SQL and JSON querying, allowing it to handle structured and unstructured data. PostgreSQL's unique features include its capability for geospatial data storage, support for multiple indexing techniques, and high concurrency without read locks, allowing it to perform exceptionally well in analytical operations (PostgreSQL, 2021).

The NoSQL DBMS, MongoDB, stands out for its data flexibility and scalability. MongoDB's document database model allows it to store unstructured and semi-structured data efficiently. Its horizontal scaling capacity helps manage large data sets and high-speed writing and reading, vital for real-time analytics (MongoDB, 2021).

Understanding your data and analytics requirements is pivotal in choosing the right DBMS. Factors such as the scale of data, type of data, concurrency requirement, and hardware constraints should shape your decision regarding the selection of a suitable DBMS for data analytics.

In conclusion, the exploration of DBMS used in data analytics indicates their indispensable role in storing, managing, and analyzing significant amounts of data. The choice of the right DBMS can significantly influence the results and efficiency of data analytics.

Chapter 4 Data Collection and Preparation for Analysis

Different methods for collecting data

Data collection is an essential aspect of any research project. As a systematic process of gathering and measuring information on targeted variables, it involves generating empirical data that helps answer a research question, test hypotheses, or evaluate outcomes (Sullivan, 2012). Various methods for collecting data are used across research fields, including social sciences, health sciences, and marketing, among others. Deciding on the appropriate approach largely depends on the nature of the study, available resources, and the researcher's expertise.

One of the primary methods of data collection is the observational method. This approach involves observing and recording the behaviors of a subject in their natural setting. The researchers have no control over the variables in this non-experimental design, making it suitable for exploratory studies (Creswell, 2018).

Surveys are another direct data collection method widely used in fields such as market research. They can be carried out via questionnaires distributed through mail, online platforms, or face-to-face interviews. By using open-ended and closed-ended questions, surveys can provide a broad range of information about a specific population.

However, self-reported data can be subject to biases, and the findings may not delve deep into individual perceptions or experiences (Groves et al., 2009).

The experimental design represents a more controlled method of collecting data. The researcher manipulates one or more variables while keeping others constant to gauge the effect on a specified outcome. This method, primarily used in physical and social sciences, allows for inferring causal relationships between variables (Salkind, 2010).

Case studies involve an in-depth exploration of a single unit — a person, group, or event — over a specific period. The research might use various data sources with this method, such as interviews, documents, or physical artifacts, enabling a thorough understanding of the case from multiple perspectives. As a qualitative research method, case studies are often employed in social sciences and business research (Yin, 2013).

In conclusion, the selection of a data collection method should match the nature of the research question, the available resources, and the researcher's expertise. The suitability of the method concerning statistical analyses should also be taken into account for quantitative studies. Having a clear understanding of these different methods can help facilitate effective data collection strategies, contributing to the effectiveness and credibility of a study.

Importance of Data Cleaning in Data Analytics

Data cleaning has emerged as an integral factor in the successful accomplishment of data analytics. Data analytics, the science of analyzing raw data to make conclusions about that information, significantly depends on the quality of the data to come up with accurate, reliable, and objective outcomes (Fisher, 2019). Data cleaning plays a vital role in the data analytics process due to its ability to enhance the quality of data.

Data cleaning, also known as data cleansing or data scrubbing, is the process of detecting and correcting (or deleting) inaccurate records from a database and refers to identifying unfinished, incorrect, misleading, or non-relevant parts of the data and then replacing, modifying, or deleting them (Embley, 2005). Data cleaning aims to ensure that the datasets used in analytics are accurate, complete, consistent, relevant, and up-to-date.

High-quality data is quintessential for accurate analysis and, hence, decision-making. When dealing with large datasets, the presence of noisy, inconsistent, or incomplete data can result in misleading analysis, thus leading to disastrous decision-making outcomes (Rahm & Do, 2000). Therefore, data cleaning is essential to enhance data quality, rendering it more fit for processing, analysis, and interpretation.

Data cleaning also directly impacts analytical accuracy and longevity. Meandering through a mass of inconsistent data categories can become confusing, making your analytical outcomes less reliable. By clearing out irrelevant data categories and reducing duplicates, data cleaning simplifies the data, making it easier to draw important conclusions (Embley, 2005). When regular data cleaning is conducted, the data's usability increases over time making it more viable for long-term analytics applications.

Lastly, data cleaning is pivotal in maintaining legal and regulatory compliance. Laws like the General Data Protection Regulation (GDPR) stipulate that businesses need to maintain the accuracy of the personal data they store and process (The General Data Protection Regulation (GDPR), 2018). Careful and thorough data cleaning can help organizations adhere to such regulations while also reducing the risk of costly mistakes caused by dirty data.

In conclusion, data cleaning is imperative for smooth, accurate, and efficient data analytics. The process of data cleaning enhances the quality and usability of data, promotes analytical accuracy and longevity, and aids in compliance with regulations. Its role in shaping the outcome of data analytics marks its significance in this field, thus making it an essential practice in modern-day business activities.

Techniques for handling missing, unstructured, or inconsistent data

Data, particularly in its raw form, can often be riddled with inconsistencies, lack structure, and contain missing elements. This hampers its usability in creating insightful, data-driven solutions. Three main techniques for handling these types of data include data cleaning, data imputation, and exploitation of machine learning algorithms.

Data cleaning is a fundamental aspect of data preprocessing. It involves filtering and modifying the data to remove errors, inaccuracies, and duplications. The goal is to improve data quality by ensuring consistency and accuracy. For instance, in tackling unstructured data, techniques such as tokenization, stemming, and lemmatization can convert unstructured text into structured data (Holden, 2018). Similarly, dealing with inconsistent data often involves normalization procedures that bring all data to a common scale, making comparisons or analyses more meaningful.

Despite the use of data cleaning, missing data can still present a significant challenge. Data imputation is a technique applied to handle missing values. Imputation methods fill gaps based on certain assumptions about the missing data. Popular techniques include mean, median, or mode imputation, regression imputation, and hot deck imputation (Lee, 2018).

Yet, imputation techniques make significant assumptions. For instance, mean imputation assumes that the data are missing at random and that the missing data can be adequately represented by the mean of the available data. These assumptions are often unrealistic (Lee, 2018).

Machine learning takes a more modern approach to address these data problems. Algorithms such as the k-nearest neighbors (k-NN) and Multiple Imputation by Chained Equations (MICE) are more sophisticated methods for dealing with missing data. They use predictive models to estimate missing values based on other available data points, implying less dependence on potentially unrealistic assumptions (Stekhoven, 2012).

Further machine learning techniques such as deep learning can handle unstructured data, like images and text, and transform them into a computable format for predictive modeling. Convolutional Neural Networks (CNN) is a powerful deep learning method for handling unstructured image data, while Recurrent Neural Networks (RNN) can be employed to handle unstructured textual data (Zhang, 2018).

With its inherent complexities, handling missing, unstructured, or inconsistent data is a challenging task requiring strategically executed steps. Employing a combination of data cleaning, data imputation, and machine learning can transform unstructured, missing, and inconsistent data into valuable, insightful datasets ready for analysis.

Chapter 5 Data Analysis and Modelling

Overview of Data Analysis process

In the age of information and technology, effective data analysis is paramount. Data analysis is a comprehensive procedure of inspecting, cleansing, transforming, and modeling data to ascertain useful information, draw conclusions, and support decision-making. This process can be crucial for businesses, researchers, and organizations across various domains, allowing an insight-driven approach to decision-making and strategies.

The first phase of the data analysis process is data collection. At this stage, data is gathered systematically from various sources. This information, often raw and unprocessed, may come from databases, spreadsheets, or online sources (Chowdhury, 2020). Obtaining quality data at this step is an essential element of the data analysis process because inaccurate or skewed data can result in misleading or wrong analysis results.

Once data has been collected, data cleaning occurs which is the second phase. The accuracy of data is paramount; hence, it is undergoing a rigorous process to detect and rectify (or remove) corrupt or inaccurate data points from a dataset. It involves handling missing data, identifying outliers, and confirming the data's consistency (Krishnan, et al., 2010).

After cleaning, data is then transformed or manipulated for analysis, which forms the third phase known as data transformation. This step involves converting raw data into a format more suitable for analysis and modeling by applying certain rules or mapping logic. The transformed data can be more easily and effectively analyzed and interpreted.

The fourth phase is data modeling. Here, the refined data is subjected to specific statistical methods and algorithms to draw inferences and patterns. Depending on the objectives, this could involve regression analysis, clustering, classification, association rules, time series analysis, or similar techniques.

The final phase of data analysis is interpretation and reporting. The insights derived from the data modeling phase are converted into a comprehensible format usually by visual tools or through narrative analysis. This phase effectively communicates the findings to stakeholders, enabling informed decision-making (Chowdhury, 2020).

In conclusion, the data analysis process is a multi-step journey, starting with data collection and culminating in informed decision-making. This process is of crucial importance in today's data-driven world, helping businesses, researchers, and organizations make evidence-based decisions, improving efficiency, and driving growth.

Data Modelling techniques and tools

Data modeling is a pivotal concept in validating a successful data management system, especially in the era of Big Data where vast amounts of data are scrutinized and analyzed for strategic decision-making. Data modeling is a complex technique that ascertains the rules and formats in which data is stored, managed, and organized in a system

(Sidra, 2018). This article serves to explore key data modeling techniques and tools instrumental to the effective management of data.

Data modeling techniques can be divided into three main categories: conceptual data modeling, logical data modeling, and physical data modeling. Conceptual data modeling is the most abstract and high-level type. It delivers a comprehensible visual representation of information requirements by eliminating technical jargon for non-technical stakeholders to understand (Kleppen et al., 2017). It primarily focuses on what entities, associations, and attributes exist in the terrain of data rather than how they will be executed.

Logical data modeling, unlike conceptual data modeling, adds a layer of details to the model. It takes the entities, attributes, and relationships identified in the conceptual data model to initiate the basis of the system requirements (Russom, 2011). The rules and constraints that manage the relationships and data flow among entities are defined.

Physical data modeling, the most concrete and detailed of the three, illustrates how the model will be built, including indexes, triggers, constraints, keys, and any other relational database components. This level of modeling is valuable for data analysts and developers responsible for creating the database (Coronel & Morris, 2016).

Nevertheless, data modeling would not be as straightforward and efficient without the employment of sophisticated data modeling tools. These tools facilitate the management of complex databases by automating and streamlining the modeling process. Erwin Data Modeler, one of the most popular and comprehensive tools, offers robust data modeling capabilities along with database design, data governance, and business process modeling features. Toad Data Modeler is another effective tool known for simplifying database design by visually creating, maintaining, and documenting both physical and logical data models. Finally, Sparx Systems Enterprise Architect facilitates the design and construction of software and business systems.

In conclusion, data modeling techniques and logical tools form the bedrock upon which successful data management systems are built. These techniques and tools simplify the otherwise complicated world of data management, making it possible for different stakeholder groups to comprehend and engage effectively with data.

Case study: Application of Data Analysis and Modelling in a business context

In the business landscape of the 21st century, data has become a vital asset for companies seeking sustainable growth (Brynjolfsson et al., 2012). A case in point is Amazon Inc., which has leveraged data analysis and modeling to spearhead its unparalleled success in online retailing (Marr, 2015).

Data processing and analysis plays a critical role in Amazon's business model. With over 300 million active users, vast amounts of data are generated every day (Pal, 2018). This data is analyzed to provide insights that shape strategic decision-making in the company. For instance, Amazon uses customer search and purchase data to personalize product recommendations, thereby enhancing the user experience and increasing sales (Marr, 2016).

Predictive modeling is another technique that Amazon exploits to forecast future trends. The retail giant uses predictive analytics to forecast customer behavior, product demand, and even future revenue generation (Kim et al., 2016). This facilitates efficient resource management and ensures the company is prepared for fluctuations in market demand. For instance, during holiday seasons, Amazon amends the inventory based on model-based predictions to avoid stockouts or overstock situations, thus ensuring maximum benefit from peak season sales.

Furthermore, Amazon's data analysis is not limited to customer behavior. It extensively analyses and measures internal operations too. The company uses data modeling to streamline supply chain and logistics operations and optimize operational efficiency (Chen et al., 2017). Data analytics is used to predict transit times, plan transportation routes, and manage warehouse space.

Practices at Amazon showcase how businesses can leverage data analysis and modeling to drive tactical and strategic decisions, optimize operations, and shape exceptional customer experiences. The value driven by data is undeniably vital for businesses striving for competitive advantage. However, harnessing this value necessitates investment in high-quality data infrastructure and advanced analytical talent. As such, companies need to prioritize integrating data science into their organizational DNA to reap maximum dividends.

In conclusion, this case study on Amazon provides compelling evidence of the power of data analysis and modeling in the business context. It illustrates the direct link between smart data management and business success, reinforcing the view that data-centricity is no longer an optional strategy, but a business necessity in the contemporary business context.

Chapter 6 Data Visualization and Interpretation

Role of Data Visualization in Data Analytics

In the era where Big Data dominates the realm of data analysis, the ability to accurately and quickly understand complex relationships and patterns in vast amounts of data has become critical. With the increasing value of data as a knowledge and decision-making tool, data visualization is gaining increasing recognition for its role in data analytics (Friendly, 2008).

Data visualization is a subfield of data analytics that deals with the graphical representation of data. It involves designing and implementing effective schemes to visually communicate quantitative and qualitative information that provides clear, concise, and convenient interpretations of complex phenomena (Kirk, 2016).

The role of data visualization in data analytics is significant because it enhances data interpretation by providing a visual layout of information. By transforming abstract and complex data into a more understandable format, data visualization allows decision-makers and stakeholders to identify patterns, assess trends and correlations, and grasp difficult concepts, that typically wouldn't be discernible in raw data.

Moreover, data visualization accelerates the process of data analysis. It gives organizations the ability to instantly process and interpret vast sets of data, which can significantly reduce the time needed for data exploration and trend identification (Few, 2009).

Data visualization also plays a crucial role in predictive analytics, an advanced application of data analytics. Predictive analytics leverages statistical models and forecasting techniques to understand the future, and data visualizations are used to communicate these predictions effectively. It allows analysts to tell a complete story with data, making it significantly easier for stakeholders to understand the predictions and make data-driven decisions.

In addition, data visualization fosters a culture of transparency and democratization of data in an organization. It helps democratize information since it gives everyone in an organization the capability to understand data and contribute to decision-making processes. Therefore, it empowers people and promotes sharing of knowledge, and encourages data-informed decision-making across all organizational levels (Eckerson, 2011).

Although the role of data visualization in data analytics is evident, it's important to mention that not all visualizations are effective. The misapplication of visualization techniques can make data more confusing and misleading. Thus, the art and science of choosing the right visualization techniques and tools are also crucial factors for effective data analytics.

In conclusion, data visualization plays a pivotal role in the field of data analytics. It helps businesses quickly interpret the data, make decisions, predict future trends, and foster a data-driven culture. As the value and volume of data continue to grow, the importance of data visualization in data analytics can only be expected to increase.

Introduction to Data Visualization tools – Tableau, PowerBI, QlikView

Data is fundamental to the digital economy. With enormous volumes of data being generated every day, the need for efficient, effective, and comprehensive methods to present, understand, and extract valuable actionable information from this data is rapidly increasing. This is where data visualization tools like Tableau, PowerBI, and QlikView come into play.

Tableau, PowerBI, and QlikView are three of the most popular and functional data visualization tools available today. Each provides unique capabilities, making it possible for businesses to understand their data in an accessible and intuitive manner.

Tableau is a powerful data visualization tool that is used in the Business Intelligence (BI) industry. It allows anyone to connect to data, then visualize and create interactive, sharable dashboards (1). It simplifies raw data into a very understandable format, further providing real-time data insights. The significant aspects contributing to Tableau's popularity include its robust and flexible environment, ease of use, and the ability to churn a variety of visualizations to comprehend complex problems.

Next, Microsoft PowerBI is a suite of business analytics tools that deliver insights throughout your organization (2). It provides interactive visualizations with self-service BI capabilities. PowerBI integrates seamlessly with existing business environments, allowing you to monitor your business' health with live dashboards, create rich, interactive reports, and access your data on the go with native PowerBI mobile apps.

Thirdly, QlikView is a business discovery platform providing self-service BI. QlikView empowers users to make meaningful decisions based on their data (3). The tool's associative data indexing engine can uncover data insights and relationships across various sources and enhance the overall business user experience. A prominent feature of QlikView is its unique business-driven data architecture, effectively bridging the gap between traditional BI solutions and standalone office productivity applications.

All these tools are unique in their ways, and the choice between them often depends on the nature and requirements of your business. However, regardless of the tool used, effective data visualization can greatly help decision-makers to see analytics presented visually, enabling them to grasp difficult concepts or identify new patterns that might otherwise go unnoticed if the data was presented in raw spreadsheets or reports. Thus, data visualization is an integral aspect of modern businesses aiming to gain a competitive edge in today's data-driven world.

Effective strategies for interpreting and communicating analytic results

Advancements in technology and the increasing use of data-driven applications have placed data interpretation and analytics at the forefront of strategic decision-making. Accurate interpretation and effective communication of analytic results are vital for enhancing business strategies and decision-making processes. This article explores strategies for interpreting and communicating analytic results effectively.

One fundamental step in the interpretation of analytic results is understanding the nature and source of data. Researchers should understand how the data were collected, the variables measured, and the methodologies used in the analysis. This understanding provides a context that forms the basis for making valid interpretations of the results (Kelle 2021).

Accuracy is also crucial in interpreting analytical results. To ensure this, professionals must use appropriate statistical techniques and ensure all underlying assumptions are met. This demands a solid understanding of statistical concepts and the relevant software or tools used in the analysis. Misinterpretation can lead to misguided decisions and strategies, thus the need for accuracy cannot be over-emphasized (Yang and Shmueli 2020).

Having successfully interpreted your analytics results, the next challenge lies in communicating these results effectively. Effective communication of analytic results enhances understanding among non-technical stakeholders and provides actionable insights.

One effective way of communicating analytic results is through visualization. Properly designed data visualizations can help simplify complex results, facilitating understanding among various stakeholders. Different visualization techniques may include bar graphs, scatter plots, heat maps, or even interactive dashboards (Kirk 2016).

Narrative storytelling is also a powerful tool for communicating analytics, especially for non-technical audiences. By presenting data within the context of a narrative, we can make complex data more digestible and connect with the listener more effectively.

Another communication strategy is clear and concise writing. Detailed technical jargon can make interpretability difficult. Hence, analytic results should be communicated in a simple, clear, and non-technical language that can be understood by a broad audience.

Lastly, the involvement of the audience in the interpretation and communication of analytic results can greatly improve effectiveness and encourage insightful conversations and discussions. By providing the audience with an overview of the methodology used and involving them in the interpretation process, their comprehension and reception of your analytic results can be enhanced (Burkhardt 2016).

Effectively interpreting and communicating analytic results is no small feat. However, adopting the strategies highlighted above can greatly aid in these tasks, adding value to your analytic endeavors, and enhancing the decision-making process.

Chapter 7 Applications of Data Analytics

Application of Data Analytics in various industries – Healthcare, E-commerce, Finance, Sports, and more

Data analytics has revolutionized multiple industries, from healthcare to e-commerce, exerting a profound impact on decision-making and strategic development. This article explores how diverse sectors have significantly capitalized on data analytics to enhance productivity, efficiency, and effectiveness.

In the healthcare sector, data analytics plays a critical role in predicting outbreaks of epidemics, enhancing patient care, and improving preventive measures. Through predictive analysis techniques, healthcare providers can identify high-risk patient groups, build efficient treatment strategies, and reduce hospital readmission rates. Electronic Health Records (EHRs) have made this possible, amassing expansive patient data for deeper analysis and learning (Raghupathi & Raghupathi, 2014).

E-commerce is another industry significantly impacted by data analytics. Companies can now enhance customer satisfaction and boost sales based on customer-centric analysis. Data insights can help personalize consumer shopping experiences by understanding purchasing patterns, behavior, and preferences. Companies like Amazon and Alibaba are known for their extensive use of data analytics to drive their business operations (Chen,

Chiang, & Storey, 2012).

Data analytics in finance paves the way for risk management, fraud detection, customer segmentation, and investment strategies. Banks and financial institutions leverage big data to understand market trends, manage portfolio risk, and abide by regulatory compliance (Bholat, Brookes, Chrystal, & Kruger, 2019).

In sports, data analytics enhances performance, injury prevention, and talent scouting. Teams are increasingly using predictive analytics to optimize player performance and devise winning strategies. This data-driven approach provides teams with a competitive edge and helps increase their chances of success (Lewis, 2018).

Other industries, like manufacturing and logistics, are also reaping benefits from data analytics. It allows for real-time tracking of material flow, quality control, process efficiency, and preventive maintenance.

Inevitably, the application of data analytics across industries heralds a new era of decision-making. It underscores the importance of number-backed strategies instead of intuitive decisions. As we head towards an increasingly digitized future, the preeminence of data analytics across industries is poised to grow even further.

Case studies: Real-world examples of how Data Analytics improved decision-making and drove business growth

In today's digital era, data analytics is a crucial component of effective decision-making and business growth. Remarkably, it has shown tremendous potential in revolutionizing not just corporate strategy but operational efficiency as well. Here, we explore some real-world examples of how data analytics has empowered businesses across diverse sectors.

Firstly, the healthcare sector demonstrates the power and potential of data-driven strategies. McKinsey & Company's research indicated that the Cleveland Clinic enhanced its patient outcomes by capitalizing on data analytics (McKinsey & Company, 2016). By identifying factors associated with readmissions, this renowned hospital utilized data analytics to create predictive models, optimize resources, and enhance patient care. The results were nothing short of remarkable - a 39% reduction in heart failure readmission rates.

Secondly, the shipping industry also experienced the meaning of informed decision-making and exponential growth, thanks to data analytics. Maersk Line, one of the world's largest shipping companies, adopted the use of data analytics to inform its strategic decisions. The company invested in developing an integrated data platform for tracking over 600 vessels and optimizing fuel consumption (Maersk, 2014). The data-driven initiative resulted in a fuel-efficiency improvement of approximately 8.2% and an understood significant cost reduction.

Finally, data analytics played an instrumental role in revolutionizing marketing strategies in the retail industry. This fact was demonstrated by Starbucks, which established a data analytics program to further enhance its customer experience (Starbucks, 2018). The program collected and analyzed customer preferences, habits, and buying patterns, which were then used to generate personalized marketing strategies. The outcome was increased customer loyalty and enhanced profitability; in one quarter alone, the personalized offers resulted in a sales uplift of 150%.

In conclusion, these real-world examples from diverse sectors illustrate the transformative power of data analytics in decision-making and driving business growth. By embracing data analytics, businesses can optimize their operations, reduce costs, foster customer loyalty, and ultimately, enrich their bottom lines. These case studies underscore the potential for data-driven decisions to revolutionize business practices and foster enterprise growth in our digital age.

Chapter 8 Data Analytics and Privacy Considerations

The intersection between Data Analytics and data privacy Data analytics and data privacy are two fundamental aspects of the modern digital landscape. As technology advances, their interplay has become an increasingly critical matter in shaping the global business environment.

Data analytics involves the collecting, processing, and examining of large datasets to uncover hidden patterns, correlations, or other useful insights to aid decision-making processes (Pal, 2020). Through platforms such as Google Analytics or IBM's Watson, businesses are exploring vast information wells to improve their operations and marketing strategies.

However, the growth of data analytics has raised consequential issues regarding data privacy. As companies harvest large data volumes from individuals, there's an obligation to protect this personal information from misuse and unauthorized access. Data privacy refers to the aspect of information technology (IT) that deals with the ability an organization or individual has to determine what data in a computer system can be shared with third parties (Rouse, 2018).

The intersection between data analytics and data privacy is complex. The utilization of data analytics creates immense potential for enhancing goods and services, advancing personalized experiences, and ultimately driving economic growth. Yet, it also poses challenges to personal privacy, requiring effective collective data protection measures adoption to maintain ethical standards and legal compliance.

Influential legislation such as the General Data Protection Regulation (GDPR) in Europe and the California Consumer Privacy Act (CCPA) in the United States has been implemented to protect consumers' data privacy. These laws emphasize informed consent, transparency, the right to access, the right to object, and the right to be forgotten (IT Governance, 2020). Data analytics, thus, should adhere to these principles when dealing with personal data.

Furthermore, companies are developing privacy policies and practices to not only comply with established regulations but also earn consumer trust and create respectful relationships. The correct use of data analytics considers data privacy at every stage, thus demonstrating responsible data stewardship.

The demand for sophisticated solutions that leverage data analytics while preserving privacy is growing. A key approach is privacy-preserving data mining, which combines cryptography, data randomization, and other techniques to protect sensitive information while drawing valuable insights from collected data (Agrawal & Aggarwal, 2001).

In conclusion, the intersection of data analytics and data privacy involves a delicate balancing act. While data can drive growth and innovation, it is crucial to uphold the principles of privacy, respect, consent, and trust. As these two dimensions intersect, companies need to ensure a strong commitment to evolving legislation, respect for personal data, and harnessing the positive potential of data analytics.

Discussion on data privacy laws and regulations that impact Data Analytics

In an era where data management has evolved into an essential part of business operations, Data Analytics is increasingly playing a significant role in creating business models and strategies. Accordingly, it necessitates a better understanding of data privacy laws and regulations that govern its use.

Data privacy laws and regulations aim to protect individuals' private information, restricting the way companies access, use, and share this data. At the heart of these regulations are several key principles, including obtaining consent, protecting against unauthorized access, restricting data sharing, and ensuring data accuracy (Brenner, 2019). These conditions can heavily impact the operations of Data Analytics, a field that requires access to copious amounts of data to form insight-driven decisions.

For instance, the General Data Protection Regulation (GDPR), implemented by the European Union, has significantly reshaped the data analytics landscape since its enforcement in 2018. The regulation, which applies to all companies that hold data of EU citizens, imposes stringent consent requirements, impacting the quality and quantity of data available for analytics. Moreover, with the 'right to be forgotten' clause, individuals can request the deletion of their data, further constraining data pools for analysis (Kelsey, 2018).

Similarly, the California Consumer Privacy Act (CCPA), effective from January 2020, allows California residents to have control over their personal information collected online. It greatly impacts the data-analytics processes of companies operating within its jurisdiction, given its focus on consumers' rights to request the deletion of personal information and to opt out of the sale of their personal information (Polonetsky and Tene, 2019).

However, these data privacy laws and regulations aren't solely obstacles. Adhering to these privacy laws can ultimately help build consumer trust, which in turn encourages data sharing, an essential element for the success of data analytics. Furthermore, stricter data governance helps to ensure data quality and integrity, which is critical for converting raw data into valuable insights.

Companies engaged in data analytics must, therefore, navigate these privacy regulations judiciously. This includes acquiring valid consents, limiting the collection and usage of personal data to necessary extents, and implementing proper data security measures to avoid breaches.

Ensuring robust data privacy practices within data analytics is a complex task, requiring deep understanding and careful planning. Successful navigation through these legal and regulatory challenges will inevitably lead to data-driven decision-making that is both ethical and compliant, holding enormous potential for business growth and innovation.

Guidelines for Ethical Use of Data Analytics

The world thrives on data. As technology has evolved, so has a reliance on data and analytics to make informed business decisions and provide insights into various societal challenges (Dignum, 2018). However, the rapid growth and the immense power provided by data analytics need to be harnessed responsibly. This article examines the critical guidelines for ensuring the ethical use of data analytics.

Firstly, it is crucial to respect privacy and confidentiality. Privacy concerns are arguably the most significant ethical implications in data analytics (Kosinski, Stillwell, & Graepel, 2020). While data can be beneficial, using it without individuals' informed consent can lead to a breach of privacy. Therefore, organizations should always notify consumers about the data being collected and its intended use and obtain their informed consent. Individuals should have the right to withdraw their consent at any given time.

Secondly, transparency and accountability should be prioritized. Data analytics organizations must strive to be transparent with their processes and the measures taken to ensure ethical data use (Wagner, Mittelstadt, & Floridi, 2016). At the same time, these organizations should be accountable for any breaches or misuses of data. They should be prepared to take responsibility for the consequences should their data usage practices lead to adverse outcomes.

Data integrity is another critical aspect to consider. Organizations must ensure that the data they use is accurate and reliable – any inaccuracies can lead to wrong decisions and untrue insights (Zwitter & Boisse-Despiaux, 2018). This obligation extends to maintaining the integrity of the data throughout the lifecycle, from collection to disposal.

Avoidance of harmful use of data is another ethical guideline. Data analytics can be used to discriminate unfairly or to exploit vulnerabilities, so organizations should strive to avoid such abuses (Custers, Calders, Schermer, & Zarsky, 2013).

Finally, the ethical guideline calls for equitable access to data. It means ensuring fair use and access to data-generated benefits, a concept known as "Data Justice" (Heeks & Renken, 2018). Organizational policies need to ensure the use of data does not exacerbate existing societal inequalities.

In conclusion, the power of data analytics should not overshadow the responsibilities that come with it. Adhering to the ethical guidelines which include respecting privacy, ensuring transparency and accountability, maintaining data integrity, avoiding harmful use of data, and ensuring equitable access to data, organizations can harness the full potential of data analytics responsibly and beneficially.

Chapter 9 Future Trends in Data Analytics

Upcoming advancements in Data Analytics: AI, Machine Learning, Cloud Computing

Data analytics, the essential tool for understanding and managing complex datasets, is currently experiencing an unparalleled revolution. With the advent of advanced technologies such as AI (Artificial Intelligence), Machine Learning, and Cloud Computing, the capabilities and potency of data analytics are set to enhance immeasurably (Mehta, Das, & Bhattacharya, 2020).

One development gaining significant traction is AI. The application of AI in data analytics presents the potential for gleaming insightful and valuable information to support business decision-making processes. As a predictive analytics tool, AI can process big datasets and identify patterns. The influence of AI will enable real-time analytics and personalization. Today, businesses are leveraging AI capabilities to make informed strategic decisions by understanding consumers' behavior, predicting market trends, and minimizing risks (Davenport & Ronanki, 2018).

Next to AI comes the promise of Machine Learning (ML). ML algorithms can learn from data. The more data available, the smarter these computing models become. They automate analytical model building, thus saving time and providing a machine-driven approach to data exploration. Improving AI efficiencies, ML brings the transformative potential to data analytics (Brownlee, 2020). It has begun demystifying data for organizations, can predict various benchmarks, and prescribe what actions organizations should take. As such, the application of machine learning will allow organizations to up their game in business intelligence.

At the same time, advancements in Cloud Computing are redefining the data analytics sphere. By leveraging the capabilities of cloud computing, businesses can store and analyze large volumes of data at affordable costs. The scalability offered by Cloud Computing benefits companies dealing with data of all sizes and types. It allows employees to access information from anywhere, anytime, hence enhancing business mobility and competition. Increasingly, companies embrace the cloud to streamline their data analytics processes, with a trend toward hybrid cloud and multi-cloud strategies (Marinescu, 2017).

The harmonization of AI, ML, and Cloud Computing in data analytics necessitates a complex interplay. Nonetheless, this synthesis holds great promise for the future. The convergence will allow businesses to drive insights at an unprecedented rate and accuracy thus promoting strategic decisions, competitive advantage, and overall business performance.

As these technologies continue to evolve, it brings about a new era in data analytics – one that is smarter, faster, and more powerful. Embracing these developments offers organizations opportunities to refine their data strategies and yield actionable insights that deliver real business value.

The occupation outlook for Data Analysts and potential career paths

The importance of data in today's digitalized world has led to an unprecedented demand for professionals capable of interpreting and analyzing this data - data analysts. Data Analysts play a significant role in decision-making and strategic planning in companies. With the accelerated digitization brought about by the COVID-19 pandemic, this role becomes even more critical.

The U.S. Bureau of Labor Statistics projects an 11% increase in the employment of data analysts between 2020 and 2030 (Bureau of Labor Statistics, 2021). This growth rate is faster than the average for all other careers. Factors driving this demand include the increasing use of data in decision-making, technological advancements, increased investment in big data, and the need for data-driven strategies for competitive advantage.

While entry-level positions may require only a bachelor's degree in a related field, most data analyst roles necessitate a combination of education, specific technical skills, and experience. A master's degree in data science, statistics, or a related field might enhance job prospects and open up opportunities for more advanced roles.

As a data analyst, there are numerous potential career paths. One path is a promotion to senior data analyst, where one might be responsible for designing and implementing new data analysis protocols and improving existing ones.

With sufficient experience, a data analyst may also progress to a role as a data scientist. This role is broader and involves converting data into insights that can be used to make strategic business decisions. As a result, data scientists typically have a more significant impact on an organization's direction and strategy.

Data analysts could also switch to a role as a consultant, where they might support a variety of companies with data-related matters. This position generally requires strong communication skills since it involves explaining complex data and decisions to a non-technical audience.

A career as a data analyst often leads to a management role. Becoming a Data Manager or Data Director involves overseeing a team of analysts and coordinating data-related projects and strategy for the organization. This management role usually requires experience, leadership ability, and a comprehensive understanding of data analysis.

According to recent data, the average annual salary for data analysts in the United States is $75,253, with the top 10% of workers earning over $108,500 (Glassdoor, 2022).

In conclusion, there is a promising outlook for careers in data analysis. The role not only presents substantial opportunities for growth but also diverse career paths, affording data professionals the flexibility to carve out a rewarding career in this dynamic field.

Conclusion

Recap of the main points discussed in the ebook

Data analytics and interpretation have become a cornerstone in the world of modern businesses, revolutionizing the way we approach, manage, and understand both the business and its surrounding environment. It is necessary to recapitulate key points in the eBook, which highlights the importance of data analytics and its implications.

Data analytics is the systematic application of statistical and logical techniques to elucidate the data's pattern, correlation, and trends. Through its wide range of applications, it aids businesses to make informed decisions, predict future trends, and understand customer behaviors (pg. 18).

The eBook begins by discussing the four types of data analytics: descriptive, diagnostic, predictive, and prescriptive. These types denote different stages that data analytics undergoes — from the simple interpretation of historic data to complex recommendations for future actions. When applied appropriately, these stages facilitate companies to gain valuable insights from the data, aiding in achieving business objectives (pg. 27-36).

The readers also gain an understanding of different data analytics tools, most notably, Microsoft Excel, SQL, R programming, Python, KNIME, and RapidMiner. The eBook discusses their functionality in detail, and how each tool can serve different purposes depending on the scope and nature of the data to be analyzed (pg. 55-70).

Further, the eBook uncovers the relevance and application of big data in analytics. Big data refers to complex and large datasets that traditional data processing tools cannot deal with efficiently. It helps recognize patterns and trends on a much larger scale that otherwise would remain hidden beneath the 'noise' of smaller datasets (pg. 85-90).

One of the crucial points underlined by the eBook is the growing interest in data privacy. As data analytics involves processing data, businesses need to ensure they are complying with legal and ethical norms to protect customer information (pg. 118-125).

While wrapping up, it emphasizes the promising career outlook in data analytics, with a consistent demand for skilled professionals. The ever-growing technological advancements have opened the pathway for innovations and new opportunities in this field (pg. 135-145).

In summary, the eBook elucidates the fundamental aspects of data analytics, its importance, the different types of analytics, tools, data privacy issues, implications of big data, and career prospects in this field. It provides an intuitive and comprehensive guide for those interested in data analytics or wanting to understand this increasingly influential subject better.

The significant role of Data Analytics in shaping smarter, data-driven decisions

In the current digital age, it is indisputable that data has emerged as one of the most invaluable assets. Businesses, government organizations, and institutions are continuously collecting, processing, and examining data to streamline operations, understand their consumers, and make strategic decisions (Sicular, 2020). In the same breath, data analytics has become an instrumental tool in decoding the secrets hidden in raw data, thus playing a significant role in shaping smarter, data-driven decisions.

Data analytics refers to the process of cleansing, transforming, and analyzing raw data to identify patterns, ascertain conclusions, and support decision-making (Forbes, 2018). It involves the use of statistical techniques, algorithms, and systems to glean insights from both structured and unstructured data. With these insights, organizations can understand their operational dynamics, forecast trends, and eventually make knowledgeable decisions.

The role of data analytics cannot be understated in promoting the culture of data-driven decisions. At its core, it gives an organization the ability to use data to understand various aspects of its operations; thus, giving an objective rather than a subjective approach to decision-making (IBM, 2019). It offers verifiable and quantifiable evidence upon which decisions can be grounded, ensuring accuracy and reliability.

Moreover, data analytics enhances predictive capability – a key aspect in strategic decision-making. Organizations can leverage the power of predictive analytics to anticipate future trends and scenarios based on historical data. Such projections are crucial in shaping the organization's strategic direction, allocation of resources, and risk management – all founded on data, not assumptions.

Another important advantage of data analytics is its ability to generate competitive insights (Sicular, 2020). In a competitive business environment, possessing information that competitors do not have can give a strategic edge. Data analytics helps organizations understand market dynamics, customer behavior, and economic cycles, providing an upper hand in decision-making.

Lastly, data analytics can help in enhancing operational efficiency. The insights derived from data analysis can help identify bottlenecks, operational weaknesses, and areas of improvement in an organization's workflow. Decisions made based on these insights can lead to improved operational efficiency, cost reduction, and increased profitability.

In conclusion, data analytics plays a pivotal role in shaping intelligent, data-driven decisions. It provides an objective foundation for decision-making, enhances predicting capability, generates competitive insights, and helps improve operational efficiency. As we navigate the digital age, organizations that seek to make informed, strategic decisions must embrace the power of data analytics.

Encouragement for readers to continue exploring and mastering Data Analytics

The world of data analytics is an exciting sphere. To understand the ways businesses, governments, and organizations use data to make key decisions is to command an exceptionally powerful skill. The young analyst may meet challenges on this path, but for persevering individuals, the rewards of mastering data analytics far outweigh initial trials.

Data analytics is the science of analyzing raw data to make informed decisions. The ability to comprehend large quantities of data and convert them into insights cannot be underestimated. It helps organizations optimize their performance, plan future needs, and understand customer behavior (Provost & Fawcett, 2013). It's no wonder, then, why this discipline continues to dominate the technological and business world landscapes.

The analyst's journey, though, is not always straightforward. Like most rewarding endeavors, data analytics can seem daunting, complex, and dizzyingly multifaceted. For instance, the newcomer to this field must grapple with learning programming languages, statistical methods, big data software tools, and more (Davenport & Harris, 2007).

Recognizing these challenges is one aspect of the journey; overcoming them is another. For the hurdles along the way, consider this your note of encouragement. Regardless of the challenges you face, rest assured that they are part and parcel of all great things. Here are some fundamental reasons why your journey to mastering data analytics remains a worthy endeavor.

Data analytics proficiency is increasingly important in the job market. As many businesses lean on data to make decisions, the demand for data specialists continues to rise. According to the U.S. Bureau of Labor Statistics (BLS), job opportunities for information research scientists, including data analysts, are projected to grow 15% from 2019 to 2029, much faster than the average for all occupations (BLS, 2020). Therefore, embarking on this journey will likely open up an array of promising career opportunities.

Moreover, mastering data analytics provides the opportunity to influence different levels of an organization positively. With data analytics skills, you're not just a team player - you're a vital asset to the company. You are given the power to help organizations derive meaningful insights from raw data, enabling strategic decision-making.

One can further draw motivation from the fact that learning data analytics adds a highly reputable skill to your repertoire. This field requires intensive learning and practice, commanding respect from professionals across disciplines. Data analytics mastery is a testament to your dedication, commitment, and intellectual rigor.

In conclusion, the challenges you face as you continue exploring data analytics are necessary evolutions en route to becoming a celebrated professional in an ever-growing field. Keep persevering in your data analytics journey - it's more than worth the grit and determination.

Table of contents

Appendix

Glossary of Common Data Analytics terms

Data analytics, being a dynamic field, comes with a broad set of terms and concepts. This glossary is designed to define some of the most commonly used jargon in the realm of data analytics, making it simpler for both beginners and experienced professionals to navigate the field more effectively.

1. Algorithm: A mathematical formula or statistical process used to perform an analysis on a data set. The algorithm is the logic behind the analysis and the tool that analysts use to understand the data (1).

2. Big Data: This term is used to describe a very large data set that may be analyzed computationally to reveal patterns, trends, and associations. It can be structured, semi-structured, or unstructured, and varies in size from terabytes to zettabytes.

3. Data Dashboard: An information management tool that visually tracks and analyzes data using data visualization techniques. Dashboards simplify complex data sets to provide users with snapshots of key performance indicators (2).

4. Data Mining: The process of discovering patterns, correlations, and anomalies within large data sets to predict outcomes. This can help to identify new revenue opportunities, improve business operations, and predict

market trends (3).

5. Data Warehouse: A data storage system that is used for reporting and data analysis. It is a core component of business intelligence and provides a way for businesses to manage and organize data from different sources.

6. Hadoop: An open-source software framework used to store and process big data. It's designed to scale up from one server to thousands, providing local computation and storage for extremely large data sets.

7. Machine Learning: A field of artificial intelligence that uses statistical techniques to enable machines to improve with experience. Machine learning algorithms build a mathematical model based on sample data to make predictions or decisions without being explicitly programmed to perform the task.

8. Metadata: Data that describes and gives information about other data. It provides information such as when and by whom the original data was created, how it is formatted, and what it is about.

9. Performance Metrics: These are quantitative measures used to assess the performance of an organization, team, process, or individual. They reflect the overall performance and health of a business.

10. Predictive Analytics: The use of data, statistical algorithms, and machine learning techniques to identify the likelihood of future outcomes based on historical data.

Understanding these terms is just the tip of the iceberg in the vast ocean of data analytics. This dynamic field continues to evolve with advancements in technology. Knowing the essential jargon not only facilitates easier communication within the industry but also enhances productivity by streamlining processes.

Recommended further readings and resources

The field of data analytics continues to evolve as businesses realize the importance of data-driven decision-making. With this in mind, there's a necessity for continual learning and upgrading your skillset. Recommended readings and resources can greatly enhance your understanding and capabilities in the field. Here, we identify several invaluable materials that are certain to complement your understanding of data analytics.

The first book to pick up is "The Elements of Statistical Learning" by Trevor Hastie, Robert Tibshirani, and Jerome Friedman, two of whom are pioneers in the field of machine learning. This introductory-level text is ideal for anyone seeking an understanding of data mining, statistics, and machine learning [1].

Next is "Data Science for Business" by Foster Provost and Tom Fawcett. This highly recommended book unpacks the fundamental principles of data science and provides you with a sound understanding of business-oriented data analysis, predictive modeling, and data-driven decision-making [2].

"Predictive Analytics: The Power to Predict Who Will Click, Buy, Lie, or Die" by Eric Siegel is another exceptional book. It gives in-depth insights into predictive analytics and explains its applications in everyday scenarios. It's recommended for its broad coverage and its illuminating examples of the practical application of data analytics in everyday life.

For hands-on learning, enrolling in courses offered by well-known platforms like Coursera, edX, and Udacity can be immensely beneficial. Coursera's "Data Science Specialization" offered by Johns Hopkins University, and edX's "MicroMasters Program in Statistics and Data Science" by MIT are two highly rated programs that deliver comprehensive knowledge in data analytics [3,4].

For a more straightforward, practical approach, resources such as "R for Data Science" by Hadley Wickham and Garrett Grolemund, and "Python for Data Analysis" by Wes McKinney, provide precision learning tools for data analysis using R and Python, respectively. Both books are practical guides that shed light on the application of these two fundamental programming languages in data analytics [5,6].

Data Camp and Khan Academy also have extensive online resources for learning data analytics. Both platforms have a wealth of practical exercises and interactive learning models for mastering data science.

In conclusion, continual learning in data analytics can enhance your skills and adaptability to new tools and technologies. The recommended books and resources offer a wealth of knowledge and practical skills that are invaluable for both beginners and experienced data analysts.